^ADam
Holds Back

Crystal Sikkens

Crabtree Publishing Company

www.crabtreebooks.com

Be An Engineer!

Designing to Solve Problems

Author: Crystal Sikkens

Series research and development:
Janine Deschenes and Reagan Miller

Editorial director: Kathy Middleton

Editor: Petrice Custance

Proofreader: Janine Deschenes

Design: Katherine Berti

Photo research: Crystal Sikkens

Production coordinator and prepress technician:
Tammy McGarr

Print coordinator: Margaret Amy Salter

Photographs:

Alamy: PNWL p16 (inset)

Shutterstock: © FashionStock.com p 3 (inset);
© FashionStock.com p10 (inset)

iStock: © mariakraynova p 6–7 (bottom); © Thaweewong p21 (right);
© doranjclark p22

Wikimedia Commons: Farwestern p12; versgui p13 (middle);
DAR56 p13 (bottom); U.S. Army Corps of Engineers p15; Stearns,
H.T. USGS p19

All other images by Shutterstock

Animation and digital resources produced for
Crabtree Publishing by Plug-In Media

Library and Archives Canada Cataloguing in Publication

Sikkens, Crystal, author
    A dam holds back / Crystal Sikkens.

(Be an engineer! designing to solve problems)
Issued in print and electronic formats.
Includes index.
ISBN 978-0-7787-2905-1 (hardcover).--ISBN 978-0-7787-2940-2 (softcover).--
ISBN 978-1-4271-1853-0 (HTML)

    1. Dams--Juvenile literature. 2. Dams--Design and construction--
Juvenile literature. I. Title.

TC540.S54 2017   j627'.8   C2016-907067-0
                                           C2016-907068-9

Library of Congress Cataloging-in-Publication Data

Names: Sikkens, Crystal, author.
Title: A dam holds back / Crystal Sikkens.
Description: New York, New York : Crabtree Publishing Company, [2017] |
    Series: Be an engineer! designing to solve problems | Audience: Ages 7-10.
    | Audience: Grades 4 to 6. | Includes index.
Identifiers: LCCN 2016055762 (print) | LCCN 2016056167 (ebook) |
    ISBN 9780778729051 (reinforced library binding : alk. paper) |
    ISBN 9780778729402 (pbk. : alk. paper) |
    ISBN 9781427118530 (Electronic HTML)
Subjects: LCSH: Dams--Design and construction--Juvenile literature. |
    Dams--Juvenile literature.
Classification: LCC TC540 .S538 2017 (print) | LCC TC540 (ebook) |
    DDC 627/.8--dc23
LC record available at https://lccn.loc.gov/2016055762

Crabtree Publishing Company

www.crabtreebooks.com   1-800-387-7650

Printed in Canada/032017/BF20170111

Published in Canada
Crabtree Publishing
616 Welland Ave.
St. Catharines, Ontario
L2M 5V6

Published in the United States
Crabtree Publishing
PMB 59051
350 Fifth Avenue, 59th Floor
New York, New York 10118

Published in the United Kingdom
Crabtree Publishing
Maritime House
Basin Road North, Hove
BN41 1WR

Published in Australia
Crabtree Publishing
3 Charles Street
Coburg North
VIC 3058

Contents

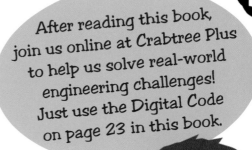

Hi, I'm Ava and this is Finn. Get ready for an inside look at the world of engineering! The Be an Engineer! series explores how engineers build structures to solve problems.

After reading this book, join us online at Crabtree Plus to help us solve real-world engineering challenges! Just use the Digital Code on page 23 in this book.

Rising River

Chelsea turned on the television and saw that heavy rains had once again filled up a nearby river. Water had begun to flow over the river's edges, and many homes next to the river had been flooded, damaged, or even washed away. Chelsea thought about the problem. What could be done to stop this from happening again?

Chelsea wondered if a mud wall could be built along the sides of the river. Or maybe a hose could be used to suck up the extra water.

Solving Problems

Throughout history, people have tried to find ways to stop rivers from flooding. One of the best ways people have found is to build a dam. A dam is a structure built across a river to hold back and collect water. The water collects behind a dam and creates a lake or pond called a **reservoir**.

Did you Know?

Some dams can be used to create power. When water passes through a dam, it makes **turbines** spin, which creates electricity.

*A reservoir can be used to water **crops**, or for fishing, boating, or swimming.*

What Is an Engineer?

Are you a problem solver like Chelsea? Do you enjoy finding solutions that can help others? If you said yes, you sound like an engineer! An engineer is a person who uses math, science, and creative thinking to design things that solve problems and meet needs.

Different Kinds

There are different kinds of engineers, including some that design computer programs, new medicine, and spaceships. Some engineers design structures, such as tunnels, bridges, and dams.

It took many years for engineers to design the Glen Canyon Dam on the Colorado River in Arizona.

Steps to Solving Problems

To find the best solution to a problem, all engineers follow the same set of steps. This set of steps is known as the Engineering Design Process. The steps in the Engineering Design Process can be repeated as many times as needed in order to make sure the solution is safe and **effective**.

The Engineering Design Process

1 ASK
Ask questions and gather information about the problem you are trying to solve.

2 BRAINSTORM
Work with a group to come up with different ideas to solve the problem. Choose the best solution.

3 PLAN AND MAKE A MODEL
Create a plan to carry out your solution. Draw a diagram and gather materials. Make a **model** of your solution.

4 TEST AND IMPROVE
Test your model and record the results. Using the results, improve, or make your design better. Retest your improved design.

5 COMMUNICATE
Share your design with others.

Asking Questions

The first step in the Engineering Design Process is for engineers to ask questions and gather information about the problem they want to solve. If engineers are trying to prevent a river from flooding, they may want to learn why and how often the river floods.

An engineer might also do research to find out what the land and **environment** is like around the river.

Brainstorming

Once engineers have gathered all the information they need, the next step is to brainstorm, or discuss with others, possible solutions to the problem.

When brainstorming, engineers might use diagrams, such as this web, to help them organize their ideas.

Create pathways that can direct the water to a safe location

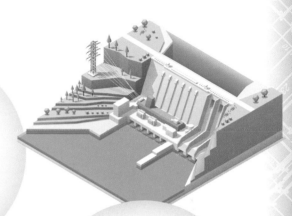

Build homes and businesses where they cannot be flooded

Problem
Heavy rains caused river to overflow and flood land, destroying homes

Build a dam

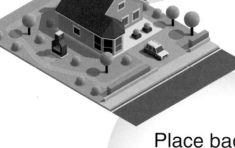

Place bags of sand next to the river

Plant trees next to the river to help block or slow the flow of water

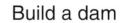

Planning

If a dam is chosen as the best solution, then the engineer must decide on the type of dam, and what materials will be used to build it. These decisions are based on things such as location, cost, and what the land is like around the dam site. Engineers choose between four main types of dams—gravity, arch, buttress, and embankment.

Did you Know?

Beavers also build dams! They use dams to hold back water in rivers and streams to create a pond where they build their homes. Beaver dams are made of sticks and mud.

*(below) Gravity dams are thick, often straight dams built of **concrete**. They must be built on hard rock.*

(right) Arch dams are thin, curved dams. They are built in narrow locations that have solid, steep rock walls. They are made of concrete and require less materials than other dams.

(left) Buttress dams are often used when the rock around the dam site is not strong enough to support the dam. They are made of concrete with a line of supports, or buttresses, that add strength to the dam.

*(right) Embankment dams are often used in wide rivers. They are built in a **sloped** shape out of hard earth and rock. Embankment dams can be built on loose rock.*

Creating a Model

Once an engineer has decided on the type of dam, he or she will create a model of it. A model is a **representation** of a real object. Some models look and work the same as the real object, but are much smaller. A model helps the team building the real dam understand the engineer's design.

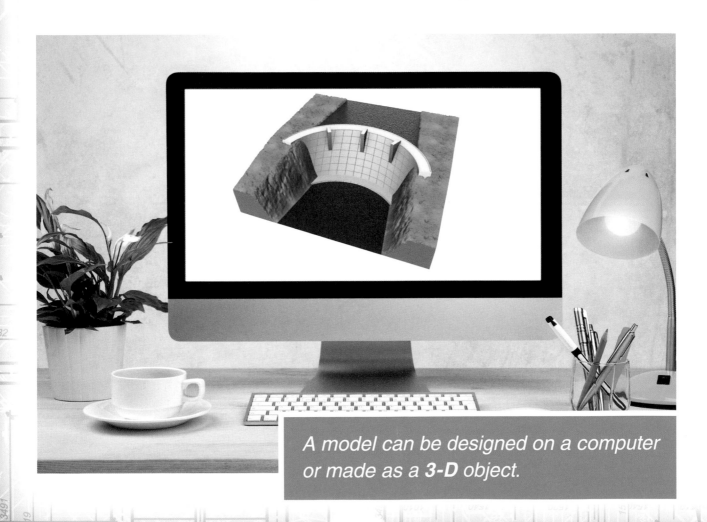

*A model can be designed on a computer or made as a **3-D** object.*

Testing and Improving

Engineers also use their model to test the design of the dam. The model helps them learn if the dam is strong enough to support the amount of **water pressure** from the river, and whether it can stand up to severe storms. After the first test, engineers record the results and then make improvements to the model. They repeat this process until the design works safely and effectively.

Testing a model will tell engineers if there are areas in their design that need fixing or improving.

Sharing the Results

Once engineers have completed the testing and improvements to their design, they share their results with others. Sharing their model and results helps engineers design stronger and safer dams in the future.

Before designing a new dam, engineers might look at past information to find out which designs worked the best.

Information from the Past

Designs of dams have changed a great deal since the first dam was built over 4,000 years ago. Thanks to information learned from the work of past engineers, today's dams are built stronger, safer, and more **eco-friendly**.

Did you Know?

There are about 850,000 dams in use around the world today.

The Three Gorges Dam in China is the largest dam in the world.

Following the Steps

Planning and building a dam correctly is very important. If an engineer does not follow the steps in the Engineering Design Process, important information could get missed and cause the dam to fail. This could destroy buildings near the dam and put many people's lives in danger.

Dam Failure

The St. Francis Dam was a gravity dam built in California in the mid-1920s. Its design was based on another dam close-by. Unfortunately, the engineer's research did not reveal that the site for the new dam was on a **foundation** of unstable rock. Because of this, the dam began to leak and eventually collapsed, or broke apart. The flood of water killed over 400 people.

These photos show the St. Francis Dam before (top) and after (bottom) the collapse.

Model Activity

The example of the St. Francis Dam has shown us that it is very important that engineers know what type of foundation their dam is being built on. Try testing this out for yourself by building and testing a model of a gravity dam.

You will need:

*modeling clay
or Play-doh*

*a rectangular-shaped
plastic container*

*gravel or
small stones*

pitcher of water

Instructions:

1. Spread the gravel to cover the bottom of the plastic container.
2. Build a dam out of clay or Play-doh. Be sure it reaches across the width of the plastic container.
3. Pour water behind the dam. Add enough water to create at least a two-inch (5-centimeter) pool of water.

- Did the water leak through the dam's foundation?
- If so, try using clay to repair the foundation and test your model again.
- What do you think would happen if you used one piece of solid rock as the foundation instead of gravel?

Avoiding Disaster

The St. Francis Dam failure was one of the worst engineering disasters in the United States. If done correctly, what steps in the Engineering Design Process could have helped stop this disaster from happening?

Many changes were made after the St. Francis Dam disaster to help make sure this would not happen again. Now, all dam designs must be approved by a team of engineers, and completed dams must be inspected regularly by an engineer.

Learning More

Books

Miller, Reagan. *Engineering in Our Everyday Lives*. Crabtree Publishing, 2014.

Nagelhout, Ryan. *How Do Dams Work? (STEM Waterworks)* PowerKids Press, 2016.

Weil, Ann. *The World's Most Amazing Dams*. Raintree, 2011.

Websites

Find out more about dams at:
http://idahoptv.org/sciencetrek/topics/dams/facts.cfm

Visit this site and put your engineering skills to work with The Dam Challenge:
www.pbs.org/wgbh/buildingbig/dam/challenge/index.html

For fun engineering challenges, activities, and more, enter the code at the Crabtree Plus website below.

www.crabtreeplus.com/be-an-engineer

Your code is:
bae04

Glossary

Note: Some boldfaced words are defined where they appear in the book.

3-D (THREE-DEE) *adjective* Short for three-dimensional, an object that has length, width, and height

concrete (KON-kreet) *noun* A hard, strong building material

crops (krops) *noun* Plants and their products that are grown and sold

eco-friendly (EK-oh-frend-lee) *adjective* Not harmful to the environment

effective (ih-FEK-tiv) *adjective* Producing the correct result

environment (en-VAHY-ern-muh-nt) *noun* The natural surroundings of things

foundation (foun-dey-SHUN) *noun* The ground or base a thing is built on

model (MOD-l) *noun* A representation of a real object

pressure (PRESH-er) *noun* The force of one thing pushing against another

representation (rep-ri-zen-TEY-shun) *noun* Something that stands in place for something else

reservoir (REZ-er-vwahr) *noun* A natural or human-made place where water is collected and stored for use

sloped (slohpd) *adjective* Slanted or tilted up or down

turbine (TUR-bin) *noun* A machine that uses moving water to create power

water pressure (WAW-ter PRESH-er) *noun* The strength of water

A noun is a person, place, or thing. An adjective is a word that tells you what something is like.

Index